Questions & Answers

OCEANS AND RIVERS

Barbara Taylor

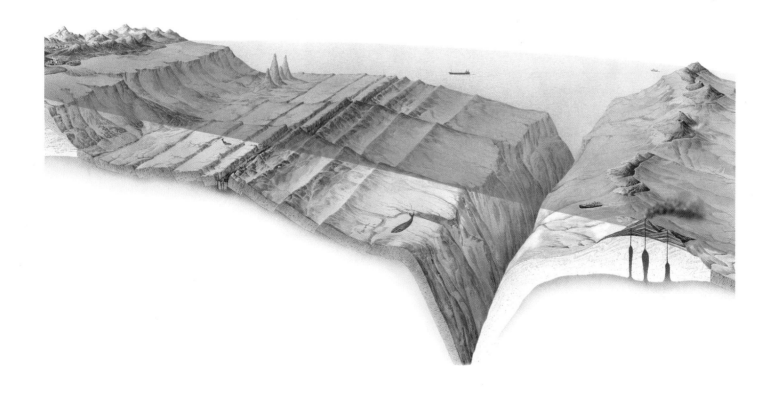

KINGFISHER

KINGFISHER
Kingfisher Publications Plc
New Penderel House
283–288 High Holborn
London WC1V 7HZ
www.kingfisherpub.com

Produced by Scintilla Editorial Ltd
33 Great Portland Street
London W1W 8QG
www.scintilla-editorial.co.uk

First published by Kingfisher Publications Plc in 2002
10 9 8 7 6 5 4 3 2 (PB)

TS/0905/TIMS/UNI(MA)/130MA/F

Copyright © Kingfisher Publications Plc 2002

ISBN 0 7534 0709 4 (PB)

Printed in China

Author: Barbara Taylor
Editors: John Birdsall, Jennie Morris and Hannah Wilson
Designer: Joe Conneally
DTP co-ordinator: Sarah Pfitzner
Artwork archivists: Wendy Allison and Steve Robinson
Production: Jo Blackmore

The publishers wish to thank Philip L. Woodworth
at Proudman Oceanographic Laboratory, Birkenhead

Contents

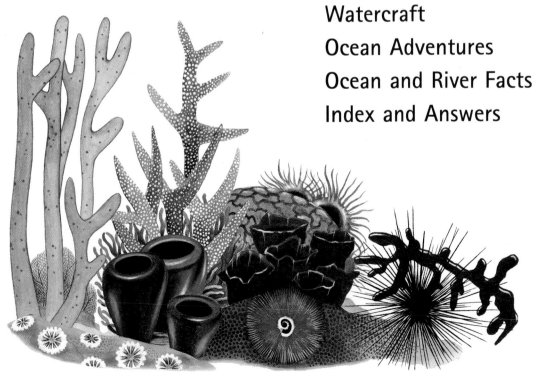

Water in Our World

Three-quarters of Earth's surface is covered by water – and nearly all of it is contained in the oceans and seas. The rest, a very small amount, is in the air or froze long ago to form the polar icecaps. Most of the water we use comes from rivers and lakes, or water that has seeped through rocks and collected underground.

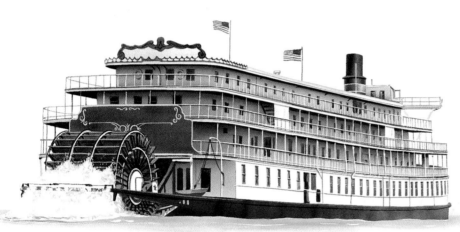

How do people use rivers?

Rivers are used for a wide range of purposes – they provide water for drinking, washing, watering crops, and large rivers are often used as highways. Transport vessels (above) carry people and cargo from place to place. Some fast-flowing rivers are harnessed to generate electricity, while others offer leisure activities, such as canoeing, swimming and rafting.

How much of the world's water is salty?

About 97 per cent of all water is the salty water of the oceans and seas. The sea is salty because salts are either washed off the land by rivers or escape from cracks in the ocean floor. Other salts come from undersea volcanoes.

— Salty seawater (97%)
— Freshwater as ice (2%)
— Fresh liquid water (1%)

What is the water cycle?

The movement of water between the land, the sea and the air is called the water cycle (right). As the Sun heats the water in oceans, rivers, lakes and plants, some of the water evaporates, which means that it changes into water vapour (a gas) and rises into the air. High in the sky, the water vapour cools and changes back into tiny drops of liquid water. This process is called condensation. The water drops gather together to make clouds and eventually fall as rain, hail or snow. The cycle then starts all over again. As a result of this recycling, the amount of water on Earth always remains the same.

Water evaporates from plants

Water evaporates from oceans and seas

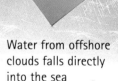

Water from offshore clouds falls directly into the sea

Do all living things need water?

Water makes up the greatest part of the bodies of plants and animals and is vital for all life. Did you know that your body is made up of more than 70 per cent water? You need to take in about two litres of water a day, and much more when it is hot or you are working hard. Aquatic animals live surrounded by water, but those that live on land have to find water (right) or get all that they need from their food.

Water vapour condenses and forms clouds

Rain, hail and snow fall from clouds

Water evaporates from lakes and rivers

Water runs off high ground

Rivers flow back into the sea

Some underground water seeps back into the sea

Why is the sea blue?

Seawater has no colour, but appears blue or green because both blue and green light from the Sun reach deeper below the surface of the water than other colours (above). The sea also reflects the colour of the sky and changes in the weather.

Why are icebergs made of freshwater?

Icebergs are chunks of ice that break away from glaciers or ice sheets – a process called calving. Icebergs are made of freshwater that falls on land as snow and is packed down, forming ice. An iceberg floats in the sea because when water freezes, it expands, making it slightly lighter than liquid water. Most of an iceberg is underwater because it only just floats (inset above). The freshwater making up an iceberg also freezes at a higher temperature than seawater, so an iceberg can be frozen while the sea is not.

Which types of creatures lived in the ancient seas?

About 500 million years ago, there were many different types of sea creature. Many would be unrecognizable today, such as trilobites (right). There were also familiar animals that are alive today, such as corals and crabs. Later, giant reptiles such as nine-metre long mosasaurs ruled the seas.

5

World Oceans

With more than 70 per cent of its surface covered by water, planet Earth could be renamed planet 'Ocean'. The relationship between water and the land has, however, been an ever changing one. Over millions of years, sea levels have risen and fallen as the climate has changed, and the pattern of land and water has altered as continents have slowly drifted apart on their own oceans of molten rock.

Which is the smallest ocean?

The Arctic Ocean is the world's smallest and shallowest ocean. It holds only one per cent of Earth's seawater – still 25 times more water than is found in all the world's rivers and lakes! The Arctic Ocean is covered by thick ice for six months of the year (right). This ice covers an area one-and-a-half times the size of Canada.

Is the Atlantic getting wider?

The North Atlantic Ocean, which separates Europe and Africa from North America, is growing wider by about three centimetres a year. This is because the continents of Europe and Africa are drifting away from North America, causing the ocean floor to crack open in the middle. Molten rock has flowed into this crack (right), producing new ocean floor, while the crust on each side of the new floor has been lifted up into a huge mountain range called the Mid-Atlantic Ridge. These mountains extend for more than 11,000 kilometres and some of the peaks stand four kilometres tall.

When part of the ocean floor slides beneath a continent, a deep trench may form.

Molten rock rises up to fill the crack in the ocean floor

How have the world's oceans changed?

Over millions of years, heat from inside Earth has made the continents drift across the surface of the globe, changing the size and shape of the oceans. About 420 million years ago, the oceans encircled four separate land masses. But by 200 million years ago, these land masses had drifted together, and a single vast ocean lapped the shores of a new supercontinent called Pangaea. Over the next 150 million years, Pangaea in turn began to break up, giving us the pattern of land and sea that we have today.

Pangaea

Which is the largest ocean?

The Pacific is the world's largest ocean, covering about one third of Earth. It is bigger than all the continents put together. The Pacific is also the deepest ocean with an average depth of 4,280 metres, but descending to 11,022 metres in the Marianas Trench off the coast of the Philippines – the deepest of all the ocean trenches. The Pacific is dotted with thousands of islands, including the Hawaiian and the Galapagos Islands. It also contains the world's largest coral reef – the Great Barrier Reef.

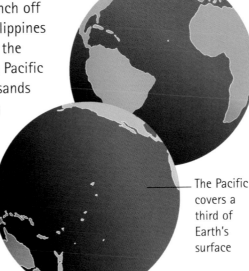

The Pacific covers a third of Earth's surface

Where two parts of the ocean floor move apart, a crack forms into which hot, molten rock wells up to make a ridge

Quick-fire Quiz

1. Which is the largest sea in the world?
a) The North Sea
b) The South China Sea
c) The Dead Sea

2. How much of Earth's seawater is in the Arctic Ocean?
a) 1%
b) 10%
c) 25%

3. In which ocean is the Great Barrier Reef?
a) Atlantic Ocean
b) Pacific Ocean
c) Indian Ocean

4. How much wider is the Atlantic Ocean growing each year?
a) 3 m
b) 3 cm
c) 13 cm

How do seas differ from oceans?

Seas are smaller areas of saltwater, usually close to, or surrounded by, land. There are about 70 seas altogether. Some, such as the Caspian are totally surrounded by land (below). Others, such as the North Sea, are only partly enclosed by land. The South China Sea, at nearly three million square kilometres, is the largest sea on Earth yet it is only a fifth of the size of the smallest ocean.

How many oceans are there?

Some geographers say that our planet has only three true oceans – the Pacific Ocean, which contains more than half the seawater on Earth, the Atlantic Ocean and the Indian Ocean. They believe that the other so-called oceans are simply part of the 'big three'. Most maps, however, not only split the Atlantic into two – the North Atlantic Ocean and the South Atlantic Ocean – but also include two much smaller oceans, the Arctic Ocean and the Antarctic, or Southern Ocean (right).

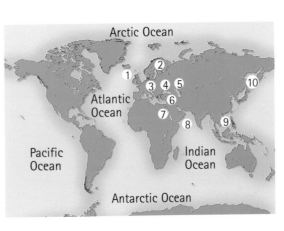

MAP KEY
1. North Sea
2. Baltic Sea
3. Adriatic Sea
4. Black Sea
5. Caspian Sea
6. Dead Sea
7. Red Sea
8. Arabian Sea
9. South China Sea
10. Sea of Okhotsk

Seas of the World

Seas are usually smaller parts of oceans – often close to, or partly surrounded by, land. The North Sea, for example, is part of the Atlantic Ocean that lies between Britain and mainland Europe. Some seas, however, such as the Dead Sea and the Caspian Sea, are really very large saltwater lakes.

How big is the Caspian Sea?

The Caspian Sea (above) is the largest inland sea on Earth, covering 422,170 square kilometres. Its surface area is more than four times that of the largest lake – North America's Lake Superior. Over the past five million years, the Caspian has sometimes been linked to the world's oceans through the Sea of Azov, the Black Sea and the Mediterranean. Today, it is quite land-locked.

Why is the Red Sea so salty?

The Red Sea contains some of the saltiest seawater in the world. This is partly because volcanoes on the sea floor add salts to the water, and also because the Red Sea is in an area with a hot, dry climate. The Sun constantly evaporates freshwater from the surface of the Red Sea into the air – leaving the salts behind. Local people often use the Sun's power in this way to extract salt for themselves (left). By building shallow pools, the speed of evaporation can be increased and the salt that is left behind can easily be raked up and collected.

What is so strange about the Sargasso Sea?

The Sargasso Sea is part of the Atlantic Ocean, between the West Indies and the Azores, where the water is very calm. Sailors used to dread this area, where they would often find themselves engulfed in thick mists, among rafts of rotting seaweed. But for the freshwater eels of North America and Europe (left), the Sargasso Sea holds a unique attraction – it is to here that they migrate to mate and spawn, before dying. Only the young eels make the return trip of up to 12,000 kilometres – miraculously managing to find their way back to the rivers their parents came from.

Freshwater eel

How has the Mediterranean Sea changed?

About six million years ago, the Mediterranean Sea was cut off from the Atlantic Ocean by rising mountains. One thousand years later, the water had all evaporated – leaving a dry sea-bed covered in salt. About a million years later, the sea level rose in the Atlantic until it began to pour over the mountains – creating the greatest waterfall in Earth's history (right). Even so, it took about 100 years for the Mediterranean to fill up completely.

How did the Dead Sea get its name?

The Dead Sea, between Israel and Jordan, is known as this because its waters are so salty that nothing lives in it for long. Its water is five times saltier than that of most oceans. Rivers flowing into the Dead Sea bring with them salt from rocks high in the mountains. The salt makes the water in the Dead Sea so heavy or 'dense' that people swimming in it float easily (right).

Quick-fire Quiz

1. Which is the world's largest inland sea?
a) South China Sea
b) North Sea
c) Caspian Sea

2. When was the Mediterranean cut off from the Atlantic?
a) 1 million years ago
b) 8 million years ago
c) 6 million years ago

3. How many more times saltier than typical seawater is the water of the Dead Sea?
a) 100 times
b) 25 times
c) 5 times

4. Which sea is the breeding place for freshwater eels?
a) Sargasso Sea
b) Dead Sea
c) Red Sea

The Ocean Floor

Hidden deep beneath the oceans lies a landscape far more dramatic than the one we see above the waves. Here, the mountain ranges are larger, the valleys deeper, the slopes steeper and the plains wider. With no wind, rain or ice to wear away the rocks, this undersea world is rough-edged and slow to change. But it is not without its own powerful forces. Ocean currents scour the sea-bed and deposit huge amounts of sediment, while fiery underwater volcanoes spout rivers of molten rock, and hot springs bubble in the depths.

How deep is the ocean?

The greatest ocean depth measured so far is the Challenger Deep, part of the Marianas Trench in the Pacific Ocean. This descends 11,022 metres below the surface – nearly seven times as deep as the Grand Canyon! The pressure at the bottom of the Marianas Trench is more than one tonne per square centimetre – a force the equivalent of 50 jumbo jets pressing down on one person!

Why do deep-sea fish glow in the dark?

More than half of all deep-sea fish glow in the dark of the ocean depths. Some produce light by means of chemical reactions inside their bodies. Other fish have bacteria inside that makes them glow – helping the fish find food and a mate, or scare off attackers in a world of perpetual night.

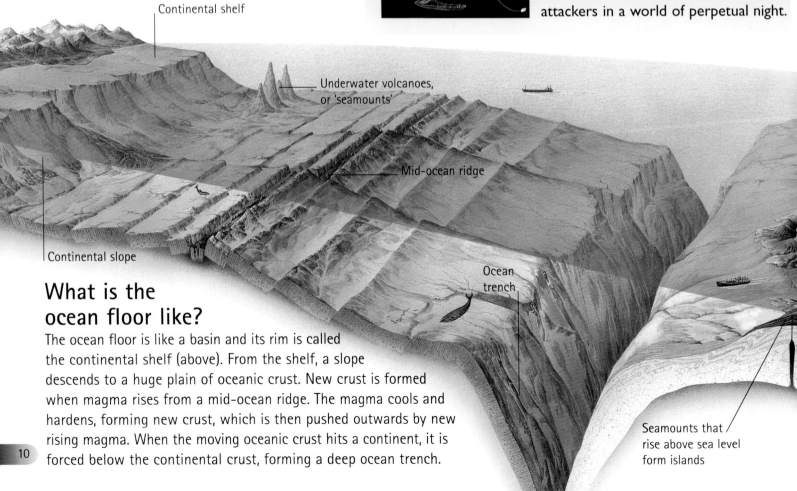

Continental shelf

Underwater volcanoes, or 'seamounts'

Mid-ocean ridge

Continental slope

Ocean trench

Seamounts that rise above sea level form islands

What is the ocean floor like?

The ocean floor is like a basin and its rim is called the continental shelf (above). From the shelf, a slope descends to a huge plain of oceanic crust. New crust is formed when magma rises from a mid-ocean ridge. The magma cools and hardens, forming new crust, which is then pushed outwards by new rising magma. When the moving oceanic crust hits a continent, it is forced below the continental crust, forming a deep ocean trench.

How do rivers create canyons under the sea?

Rivers wash huge amounts of sediment into the sea, where it builds up on the continental shelf – the shallow ledge surrounding the land. If this sediment piles up too high, or is disturbed by an earthquake, it may begin to move. This results in a 'turbidity current' – a massive amount of water and sediment that slides across the continental shelf. Turbidity currents can travel at up to 90 km/h and have huge erosive power, carving out narrow, steep-sided canyons in much the same way as rivers do on land.

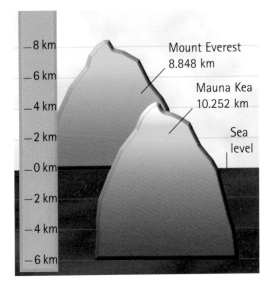

A turbidity current carves out a canyon as it flows downhill

Which is Earth's tallest mountain?

Even though Mount Everest is considered to be the tallest mountain on Earth, there is an underwater mountain that is even bigger. Mauna Kea, a gigantic volcano in the Pacific Ocean rises an incredible 10.252 kilometres from the sea-bed (right) – more than 1,000 metres taller than Mount Everest! The 4.205 kilometres of Mauna Kea that is above sea level forms the tropical island of Hawaii. Mauna Kea means 'white mountain' in Hawaiian because its peak is often snowcapped.

—8 km
—6 km
—4 km
—2 km
—0 km
—2 km
—4 km
—6 km

Mount Everest 8.848 km
Mauna Kea 10.252 km
Sea level

What are black smokers?

In the darkness of the ocean, some 3,000 metres down, chimneys spew out what looks like black smoke. These chimneys form when boiling hot water gushes up through cracks (deep-sea vents) in the sea-bed. The hot water spurting out of the top of the chimneys is black with mineral-rich particles. Some of these minerals are deposited around the vents, building up to form tall chimneys. Black smokers occur near mid-ocean ridges where two plates are pulling apart. Giant tube worms, clams and other strange marine creatures live in the mineral-rich waters around black smokers.

Islands and Reefs

Islands form in many ways. Those near the shore may be chunks of land that have broken away from a continent, or simply parts of the mainland cut off by rising sea levels. Ocean islands, far from any land, are usually the tops of underwater volcanoes. Coral islands called 'atolls' are the remains of reefs around submerged volcanoes.

How do coral atolls form?

1 Coral often grows on the shores of volcanic islands where the water is shallow, warm and rich in minerals. Over hundreds or thousands of years, the island may sink or the sea level may rise.

2 The coral grows together with tiny plants called algae, which need sunshine to develop. So, the reef constantly grows upwards towards the Sun.

3 When the island finally disappears beneath the waves, a deep ring of coral, or 'atoll', which surrounds a shallow central lagoon, is left behind.

Is coral a plant or an animal?

Coral looks like a plant, but is, in fact, a tiny animal called a polyp. Related to jellyfish and sea anemones, polyps are soft, delicate animals with tentacles that capture small particles of food from the seawater. To protect themselves from predators, many corals build hard, stony shells around their bodies (left) and when the polyps die, these cases are left behind. Over time, millions of these empty cases build up to form coral reefs. Even though the bottom of a reef may be dead, the surface is very much alive.

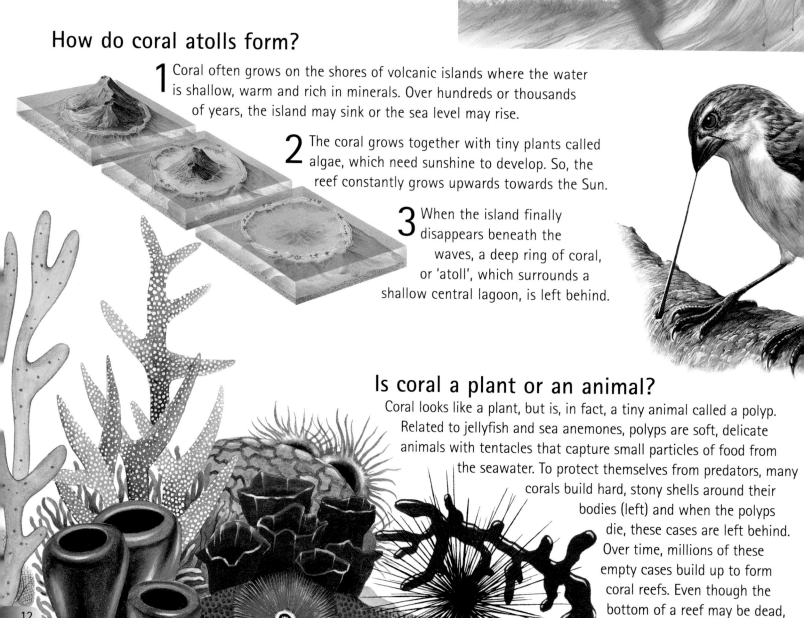

How do volcanoes form islands?

Underwater volcanoes are formed when magma forces its way through weak spots in the ocean crust. When the lava meets the cold water, it solidifies. Over time, this rock builds up to form an undersea volcano. If the volcano grows big enough, it breaks the surface and an island is born. The Galapagos Islands, the Hawaiian Islands and the island of Surtsey, which appeared off the coast of Iceland in 1963, were all formed in this way. When a volcanic island erupts, it can cause huge waves called tsunamis (left).

Which is the largest coral reef?

Off the east coast of Australia, stretching more than 2,000 kilometres, the Great Barrier Reef is the biggest coral reef in the world. It is also the largest structure made by any living thing – it is so big it can be seen from space! Corals only grow about 15 centimetres every year, so parts of the Great Barrier Reef are approximately 18 million years old.

Great Barrier Reef

Australia

Quick-fire Quiz

1. What are corals closely related to?
a) Sponges
b) Sea squirts
c) Sea anemones

2. How much does coral usually grow in a year?
a) About 15 m
b) About 15 cm
c) About 15 mm

3. Which volcanic island appeared in the North Atlantic in 1963?
a) Iceland
b) Surtsey
c) Hawaii

4. About how old is the Great Barrier Reef?
a) 200 million years
b) 8 million years
c) 18 million years

Why is island wildlife so special?

Islands may form in different ways, but they all have one thing in common – they are relatively isolated. As a result, they are often home to unusual animals that are found nowhere else. It was the unique ways in which finches had developed on the Galapagos Islands – the woodpecker finch uses cactus thorns to spear insects (left) – that helped Darwin develop his theory of evolution.

Why are coral reefs so rich in wildlife?

One third of all types of fish live on coral reefs, which are rivalled only by rainforests for their 'biodiversity' – their variety of nature. In the warm, sunny waters of the reef, food is plentiful, and the nooks and crannies provide shelter for predators and prey alike. Large reefs are also millions of years old, allowing time for a complex web of life to develop.

Ocean Currents

Ocean currents are like huge 'rivers' of water that flow through the sea, either at or near the surface, or far below, close to the sea-bed. They are driven by winds, differences in water density, and affected by the depth and shape of the sea-bed and the spin of Earth. One of the largest currents – the West Wind Drift – carries 2,000 times more water than the Amazon, the largest river in the world. Ocean currents have an important influence on climate and ocean transport.

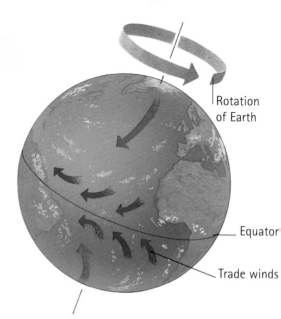

Rotation of Earth

Equator

Trade winds

What is the 'Coriolis effect'?

Named after French mathematician Gustave Coriolis, the 'Coriolis effect' is produced by the rotation of Earth and has a direct bearing on wind and ocean-current patterns. Because Earth is spinning anti-clockwise, winds and ocean currents travelling from either pole to the equator are deflected significantly westwards (above).

 Cold surface currents    Warm surface currents

What do ocean currents carry?

Ocean currents once carried little more than unusual plant life. While seeds from South America still turn up in the UK – due to a current called the Gulf Stream – most debris is of human origin (below). Debris can sometimes provide valuable information about the speed and direction of currents. When 80,000 pairs of trainers were swept off a ship travelling between South Korea in Asia and Seattle, USA, an international study monitored when and where they finally washed up.

What causes surface currents?

Currents in the top 500 metres of the ocean are called surface currents. They are caused by the wind and usually travel at about ten kilometres a day. They are deflected by the spin of Earth, which makes them flow clockwise in the northern hemisphere and anti-clockwise in the southern hemisphere. Cold currents flowing from the polar regions replace warm currents deflected away from tropical equatorial regions (above). Earth's spin, together with the shapes of the continents, makes the surface currents flow in five gigantic loops called gyres.

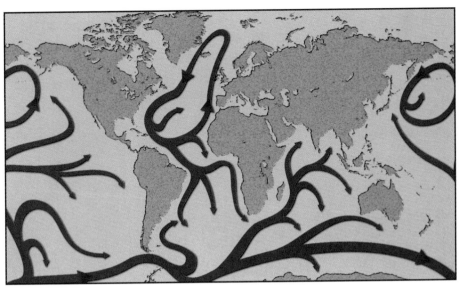

What are deep ocean currents?

In the polar oceans, cold, very salty water sinks to the ocean floor and flows along the sea-bed towards the equator as a deep ocean current. As it warms up, it becomes lighter than the surrounding water, so it rises to the surface. It then flows back to the poles again, as a warm surface current. This circular movement of water (left) means that eventually all the water in the oceans will relocate – but it can take 1,000 years for deep-sea water to return to the surface.

What is El Niño?

Off the coast of Peru, South America, cold water usually rises up from the ocean depths, bringing with it a rich supply of nutrients that provide food for millions of fish and birds. Every two

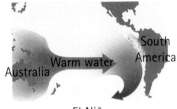

Australia / Warm water / South America

El Niño

Pacific Ocean

Cold water

Normal Conditions

to ten years, however, the winds change, and a warm water current, called El Niño, displaces the cold, nutritious current. With their food supply cut off, huge numbers of fish and seabirds die. El Niño also disrupts the weather, often causing serious flooding in Ecuador and Peru.

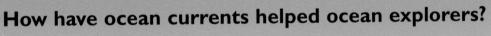

How have ocean currents helped ocean explorers?

In 1947, the Norwegian explorer Thor Heyerdahl, sailed a balsa-wood raft called *Kon-Tiki* from Peru to the Tuamotu Islands in the Pacific. During a voyage that lasted four months, the raft covered 11,300 kilometres, using the South Equatorial Current to help it on its way. Heyerdahl hoped that his adventure would prove that early South Americans could have reached the Polynesian Islands long before settlers arrived from the West.

Oceans and Climate

The oceans have a major effect on Earth's climate, soaking up the Sun's warmth and transporting heat from the equator towards the poles by means of ocean currents. Winds blowing over the oceans are warmed or cooled by the water, and these winds then raise or lower temperatures on land. The oceans also release vast amounts of moisture into the air, which may fall later as rain or snow.

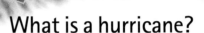

What is a hurricane?

Fierce, whirling storms called hurricanes can be up to 600 kilometres wide, with destructive winds spinning up to 170 km/h. Hurricanes (right) start over oceans near the equator, where two air masses meet and the ocean temperature is at least 25°C. Warm, moist air is drawn up from the ocean's surface in a slow, circular motion caused by Earth's spin. The hurricane draws more and more warm air from below – making the storm grow. Over land, the storm is cut off from the warm air that drives it, and eventually loses its power.

Sun's heat enters atmosphere

Some radiated heat escapes

Heat reflected back to space

Radiated heat trapped by greenhouse gases increases Earth's temperature

Are sea levels rising?

Sea levels rise and fall as Earth's temperature increases or decreases. Warmer temperatures cause the ocean waters to expand and some of the polar icecaps to melt, making sea levels rise. This is because sea levels are related to the amount of water locked up in snow and ice. Due to global warming, caused by the greenhouse effect (left), sea levels are rising – and by the year 2100 they may have risen by 45 centimetres. Such an increase would drown hundreds of coral atolls and threaten cities such as New York.

What is a waterspout?

A waterspout is a whirling tornado that forms over warm, tropical waters, such as those in the Gulf of Mexico. Unlike a hurricane, which grows from the surface of the sea upwards, a waterspout begins as a rotating funnel of air extending downwards from a thunder cloud (right). As it touches the surface of the sea, water is sucked up to form a column that can extend 10 metres across and up to 120 metres high.

Why is San Francisco often foggy?

Sea fogs form when warm, moist air moves over cold water, causing the vapour in the air to condense into a fine mist. The California Current off the coast of San Francisco carries cold water south from the Arctic. When warm, moist air moves over this water, a dense fog forms – shrouding the city and its famous Golden Gate Bridge (above).

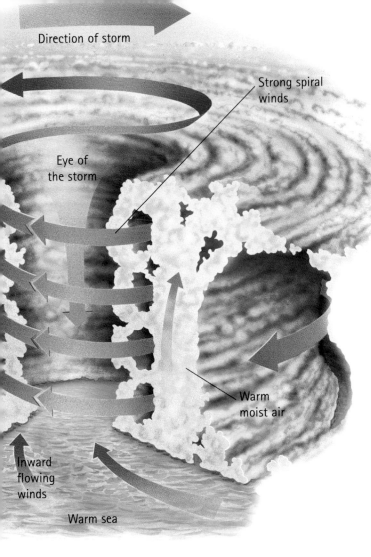

Direction of storm

Strong spiral winds

Eye of the storm

Warm moist air

Inward flowing winds

Warm sea

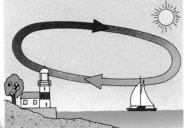

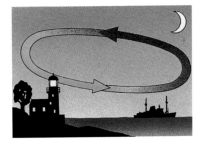

What are land and sea breezes?

Coastal winds that blow onto the land by day, and out to sea at night, are called land and sea breezes. They occur because the sea warms up and cools down more slowly than the land. During a sunny day (above left), the land heats up faster than the sea, so warm air rises off the land and a cool breeze is sucked in from the sea. If the night is clear (above right), the land cools down faster than the sea. As warm air rises over the sea, it draws the cooler, land air out over the water.

Quick-fire Quiz

1. Which country has a lot of fjords?
a) India
b) Norway
c) Australia

2. How many gates has the Thames Barrier?
a) 5
b) 10
c) 12

3. What affects sea levels most?
a) Earth's temperature
b) The Sun
c) The Moon

4. Where do hurricanes form?
a) Over warm, tropical oceans
b) Over cold, polar oceans
c) In the North Sea

What is the Thames Barrier?

London's Thames Barrier can seal off the upper part of the River Thames from the sea – protecting the capital from storm surges and very high tides. The barrier consists of ten movable gates, each as high as a five-storey building, supported between concrete piers. The gates usually lie flat on the river-bed, but they can be rotated 90 degrees to the vertical at the first sign of dangerously high water.

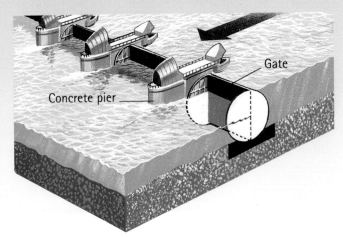

Gate

Concrete pier

What are fjords?

About 10,000 years ago, during the last ice age, glaciers carved out long, deep valleys along the coasts of countries such as Norway. As the ice melted, and sea levels rose, these U-shaped glacial valleys were flooded to form long, steep-sided inlets called fjords (below).

Waves and Tides

Most waves are caused by the wind. The faster the wind and the longer it blows – the larger the waves. Volcanic eruptions or earthquakes can also produce destructive waves that can reach 30 metres high. The more gentle rising and falling of the tides is caused by the pull of gravity from the Moon and the Sun. The highest tides occur in the Bay of Fundy, Canada, where the sea can rise higher than a four-storey building in just six hours.

How do waves work?

Unlike currents and tides, waves do not move water along. The waves travel, but the water within each wave stays in almost the same place – moving round in circles. Long after the wind that created them has died away, waves can travel long distances. Waves that break on the Pacific coast of the USA may have begun 10,000 kilometres away.

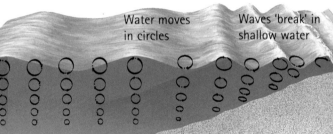

Water moves in circles

Waves 'break' in shallow water

What causes tides?

On most coasts, the sea rises and falls twice a day. High tide is when the water is 'in' and low tide is when the water is 'out'. Tides are caused mainly by the pull of the Moon's gravity. The Moon pulls the water in the oceans nearest to it outwards. At the same time, because Earth is spinning, the oceans on the opposite side of Earth are also pulled outwards. These two bulges in Earth's oceans correspond to high tides, while the oceans in between are at low tide. Tides change (rise or fall) as Earth spins and the position of the Moon alters.

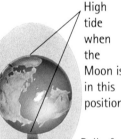

High tide when the Moon is in this position

Pull of the Moon

The Moon orbiting Earth

What happens to waves when they reach the shore?

As a wave nears the shore, the sea is too shallow for the water inside it to make a circle (top right), so the crest of the wave topples over and the wave breaks – releasing the energy stored up during its journey. Surfers (left) try and stay just ahead of this breaking crest. If the sea-bed slopes gently, waves break before reaching the shore, but where it is steeper the waves surge on to the shore. The foaming water that runs up the beach is called swash and the water returning to the sea is called backwash.

What are spring and neap tides?

The Sun's pull on Earth's oceans is weak because it is so far away. But twice a month, when the Sun, the Moon and Earth are in line (below left), the pull of the Sun and the Moon combine to produce higher high tides and lower low tides than usual. These 'spring' tides happen at Full and New Moon. When the Sun, the Moon and the Earth form a right angle (below right), the Sun's pull works against the Moon, producing low high tides and high low tides. These 'neap' tides happen when the Moon is in its First and Last Quarter.

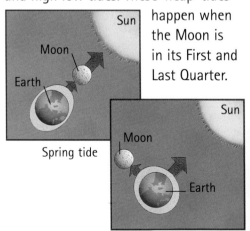

Sun

Moon

Earth

Spring tide

Sun

Moon

Earth

Neap tide

How can waves and tides generate electricity?

Water is a valuable source of energy. On coasts where the tidal range is over five metres, a tidal barrage, or barrier, harnesses the energy in waves to rock huge floats. These floats absorb the energy and use it to drive pumps. The pumps force liquid through turbines, which generate electricity.

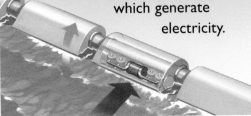

What is a tsunami?

Waves that are triggered by undersea volcanoes or earthquakes are called tsunamis. These are far more powerful than the waves produced by the wind because tsunamis cause all the water from the sea-bed to the surface of the sea to move. In the open ocean, these waves appear small, but they travel vast distances at the speed of a jet. When they approach land, they slow down and grow into a terrifying wall of water 30–50 metres high (below). The largest recorded tsunamis have been more than 280 metres high.

How do waves and tides affect wildlife?

Waves can pound, crush or dislodge shore creatures from their hiding places. Tides expose them to predators, such as birds (below), and to the Sun and wind. So animals that live on the shore must be resourceful. Some burrow beneath the sand for safety, while others hide in pools or among the rocks. Many have special adaptations, such as the conical, wave-resistant shells of limpets.

Quick-fire Quiz

1. What is the main cause of ocean tides?
a) The Moon's gravity
b) The Sun's gravity
c) Earth's rotation

2. What are spring tides?
a) Higher and lower tides than usual
b) Tides that happen in spring
c) Tides that come in really quickly

3. What causes a tsunami?
a) Undersea volcanoes or earthquakes
b) Very strong winds
c) Hurricanes

4. Which animal has a conical shell to resist the waves?
a) Mussel
b) Clam
c) Limpet

Coasts

The world's coastlines stretch for about 500,000 kilometres – long enough to circle the equator 12 times. Despite this great length, almost every coastline is different. This is because the shape of the coast depends on the kind of rock it is made of, and how it is shaped by the waves and the wind. Some coasts are steadily being added to, while others are being eroded by the relentless action of the wind and waves.

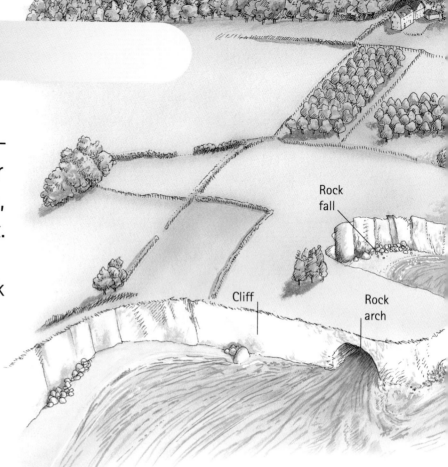

Rock fall

Cliff

Rock arch

What lives in rock pools?

Safely hidden under water in a rock pool (below), a wide variety of coastal wildlife can wait for high tide. Sea anemones and shellfish cling to the rocks, while crabs, shrimps and prawns scuttle about, and sea urchins scrape away at plants with their powerful teeth. Rock pools can be difficult places in which to live. Exposed to the Sun, wind and rain, the temperature, acidity and saltiness of the water can vary enormously. The oxygen and carbon dioxide levels can also fluctuate, with often disastrous consequences for the pool's inhabitants.

How do we protect the coast?

About 60 per cent of the world's population lives within 60 kilometres of the coast and over two-thirds of the world's cities, with populations greater than one million, are by the sea. Huge numbers of tourists also take their holidays on the coast. Many coastlines are protected by sea walls, groynes and artificial beaches. But natural coastlines are constantly changing and, when we try to protect the coast and keep beaches from being washed away, it often causes problems elsewhere along the coast.

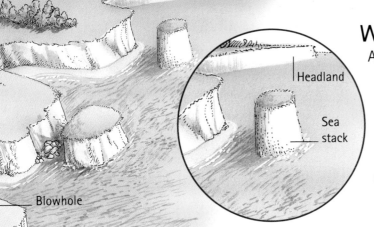

Headland

Sea stack

Blowhole

What is a sea stack?

A tall pillar of rock just off the coast is called a sea stack (left). It starts to form when waves cut away caves on both sides of a headland. Eventually, the caves meet in the middle and a rock arch is formed. The waves continue to lap around the arch, steadily widening it until the roof collapses, and an isolated sea stack remains.

How do waves wear away the coast?

The main way in which the sea wears away, or 'erodes', a coast is by hurling sand and pebbles against it. The sheer force of the waves also helps to break the rocks up into smaller pieces. Where the coast is being eroded by the sea in this way there are bays, cliffs and headlands (left). The world's highest sea cliffs are in Hawaii. They are over twice the height of the Empire State Building in New York!

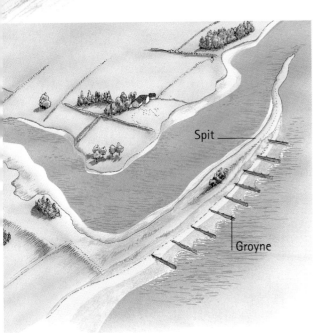

Spit

Groyne

What is a spit?

When a coastline curves or changes direction, longshore drift (below) may wash sand and shingle out to sea – forming a long, snake-like ridge called a spit (left). The tip of a spit often curves towards the land because the waves push beach material in that direction. If a spit grows across the mouth of a bay, it may eventually reach the mainland on the other side – cutting off the bay from the open ocean. The spit is then called a bay barrier. If an island is joined to the mainland by a spit, the spit is called a 'tombolo'.

What is longshore drift?

On some coasts, the sand or shingle is moved along the shore by the waves (right). This is called longshore drift and it happens when the waves hit the beach at an angle, before falling back down the beach in a straight line. As the waves follow this zig-zag path along the coast, they take some of the beach with them. Sea walls called groynes are often built to trap the sand and stop it drifting away.

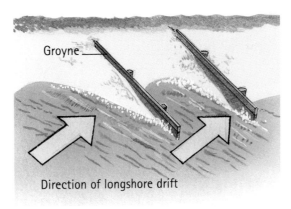

Groyne

Direction of longshore drift

A River's Journey

Rivers contain less than one per cent of all the freshwater on Earth, yet they are a powerful force in shaping the land. Over thousands of years, rivers can wear away the rocks they flow over, and carve out broad, flat-bottomed valleys. They also carry away rocks, sand and sediment, depositing them in lakes, under the sea or over the land, making rich farming soil.

How do rivers start?

The beginning, or source, of a river is often just a natural hollow in the ground. Rainwater trickles in from the surrounding soil to start a flow of water. Even huge rivers, such as the Nile and the Amazon, start from tiny beginnings like this. Other rivers are fed by underground springs or flow from marshes, lakes or glaciers.

Tributary

Flood-plain

Meander

Ox-bow lake

Estuary

What are meanders?

Rivers rarely flow in a straight line, but twist and turn in loops called meanders (above). Meanders begin when the river tries to flow around a shallow part of its bed called a riffle. As the water swings to one side, it cuts into its bank. As this cut deepens, it becomes a shallow bend. Some of the eroded material is deposited on the inside of the bend and forms a small beach. Over time, the cut becomes deeper and the beach becomes larger – producing a snake-like bend in the river.

How do rivers wear away the land?

Rivers usually cut into the land by 'abrasion' (left) – they scratch and scrape at the river-beds with the rocks and sediment that they carry. Where river-water swirls pebbles round and round, pot-shaped holes may form on the river-bed. Rivers are most powerful in flood conditions when the increased volume of water sweeps huge amounts of soil and large rocks downstream. Rivers can also dissolve some rocks, and carry them away in solution.

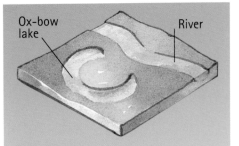

Ox-bow lake   River

Rain falls on high ground

River begins as small mountain stream

Rivers join as they flow to the sea

How is an ox-bow lake formed?

Once a river has begun to meander, the snake-like curves steadily become more extreme, as the water swings powerfully into the outside of the bend and drops more sediment on the inner side. Over time, the neck of a meander can become quite narrow. If the river floods, it may cut through this neck, leaving the meander behind as an 'ox-bow lake'.

Quick-fire Quiz

1. What is a shallow part of a river-bed called?
a) A rapid
b) A riffle
c) A weir

2. Which lake is one of the sources of the Nile?
a) Lake Superior
b) Lake Margaret.
c) Lake Victoria

3. How much shorter than the Nile is the Amazon?
a) 596 km
b) 680 km
c) 255 km

4. What kind of lake is formed from a meandering river?
a) An oxtail lake
b) A horseshoe lake
c) An ox-bow lake

How is the otter adapted to live in rivers?

The otter is a superb swimmer, with webbed feet, a streamlined body and a muscular tail for steering through the water (above). When swimming slowly, it uses a kind of doggy-paddle. But by flexing its whole body up and down like a seal, the otter can reach speeds of up to ten km/h. To stay warm and dry in even the coldest of rivers, the otter has two layers of fur. The outer layer of 'guard hairs' is waterproof, while a dense, fine underfur traps air to keep the otter warm.

Which is the world's longest river?

Nile delta
Khartoum
Blue Nile
White Nile
Ethiopia
Lake Victoria
Atlantic Ocean
Indian Ocean

Flowing 6,695 kilometres through north-east Africa, the Nile (left) is the world's longest river – with the River Amazon a close second, just 255 kilometres shorter. The Nile has two main sources – the White Nile, which flows from Lake Victoria, and the Blue Nile, which flows from the Ethiopian highlands. The White and Blue Niles join at Khartoum in the Sudan, and from there it flows north to the Mediterranean, where it ends in a vast triangular delta. Much of the river's course is through desert, where it brings life to the parched landscape.

River Landscapes

A river is said to have youth, middle age and old age. According to its age, it changes the landscape in different ways (right). In its youth, near its source, it races over waterfalls and rapids, scouring a deep valley. Downstream, in middle age, it slows, losing its cutting power – it begins to meander, or wander, spilling on to a plain in times of flood. In old age, the river widens as it nears the sea, forming an estuary, and the flow slows down.

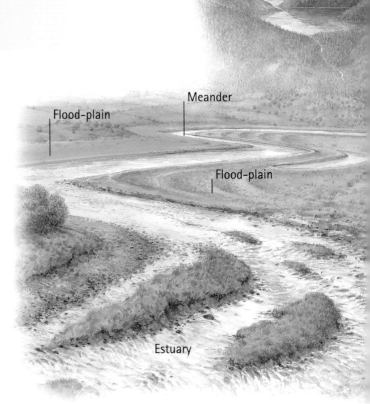

Flood-plain

Meander

Flood-plain

Estuary

What are river canyons?

Some rivers carve long, deep valleys called canyons – especially where the climate is very dry. Here, rain falls in sharp, heavy bursts. There is little soil and few plants to soak up the water and it rushes over the land, cutting downwards with great force. The Grand Canyon (left) in North America is more than 450 kilometres long, and about 1.5 kilometres deep.

Why are river valleys V-shaped?

Close to a river's source, its valley is narrow and steep-sided (left). This is because the fast-flowing water sweeps along pebbles and grit, which act as powerful abrasives. In this way, the river cuts downwards faster than it cuts sideways and makes a V shape.

Waterfall

Rapids

What is a drainage pattern?

The way that rivers and streams all join up in an area is called a drainage pattern, and there are several different types. A dendritic drainage pattern, for example, looks like the branches of a tree – the River Amazon has this sort of drainage pattern (right). Some other patterns are called radial, trellis and parallel patterns.

Where is the highest waterfall in the world?

The highest waterfall is Angel Falls (right), in Venezuela, South America. Here, water from the River Carrao plunges over a sheer cliff for 807 metres in a single drop before hitting a rocky outcrop. It then tumbles a further 172 metres before hitting the base, giving a total drop of 979 metres – more than three times the height of the Eiffel Tower!

Eiffel Tower
300 metres

What is a flood-plain?

A flood-plain (above) is the wide, flat valley near the end of a river's course. Here, it is easy for a river to break its banks in times of flood, spilling water and mud over the flood-plain and creating good soil for farming (left).

How is a waterfall made?

1 When a river flows over bands of hard and soft rock, the soft rock wears away first, leaving a slight step.

Soft rock   Hard rock
          Soft rock

2 The soft rock below the step wears away more quickly because the water falls with greater force onto it.

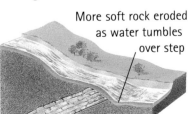

More soft rock eroded as water tumbles over step

3 In time, the water scours a deep pool below the hard rock step. Now, the water has to fall over the lip of the step.

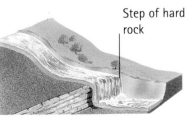

Step of hard rock

25

Where Rivers Meet the Sea

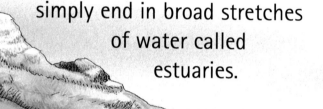

Delta shape

Arcuate delta

Most rivers end their long journey at the sea. Here the river's flow slows down and its heavy load of sediment is finally allowed to settle. On the coast, if the tides are strong enough, some of this sediment is washed out to sea. But some of it may build up into a new piece of land called a delta. This word comes from 'Δ', the symbol for the Greek letter 'd', which is the same triangular shape. Many rivers, however, simply end in broad stretches of water called estuaries.

What shape are deltas?

The shape of a delta depends on how much water and sediment is carried by the river, and how fast it is flowing. It also depends on the speed and strength of the waves, currents and tides on the coast. An arcuate delta (above), such as that of the Nile, Indus or Rhône, forms where waves, currents and tides are weak. A cuspate delta, like that of Italy's River Tiber, ends in a point or peak. Here, strong waves force the sediment to spread out in both directions from the river's mouth. A bird's foot delta, like that of the Mississippi, forms when a lot of sediment is carried out into calm seawater.

Lake

Estuary

Sea

What is a river estuary?

An estuary is the broad area of water where a river meets the sea (right). It is a place of constant change. At low tide it is a freshwater environment, but at high tide it becomes increasingly salty. Estuaries are also muddy places because the river slows down as it meets the sea and releases the sediment it is carrying. The seawater makes the mud and silt clump together and drift to the bottom. Huge numbers of worms and shellfish live in this rich mud, providing food for many birds.

Why do flounders have both eyes on one side?

Flounders (right) are a kind of fish that have developed flattened bodies so that they can lie hidden among the sand and silt of the river-bed or sea-bed. Because they lie on one side, they have both eyes on the other – usually the right side. When they start life, however, they look like most other fish, with one eye on either side of the head. As they grow, one eye moves to the same side of the head as the other eye. The nostril and the mouth also move to this side of the head. Flounders are typical estuary fish, migrating up rivers to feed in summer and returning to the sea to breed in autumn.

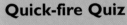

Why are mangroves unusual?

Mangrove trees are unusual because they are specially adapted to live in wet, salty and muddy swamps. Their stilt-like, arching roots (left) trap mud brought down to the sea by rivers, and help to transform coastal swamps into dry land. They grow so densely that they help to protect the coast from storms and floods. Mangroves are also odd because they 'breathe' air through their arching roots. They need to do this because there is little oxygen in the wet mud. The seeds that mangroves produce start to grow on the tree, which increases their chance of survival when they drop into the mud below.

Why is quicksand dangerous?

Quicksand is usually found in hollows at the mouth of large rivers, or along flat stretches of sandy beaches. It forms where a permanent pool of water becomes filled with sand and sediment. The sand is so waterlogged that it cannot support any weight and it behaves like a liquid. If a person steps on to an area of quicksand, they may be sucked beneath the surface and eventually drown.

Quick-fire Quiz

1. What is the water like in a river estuary?
a) Salty
b) Fresh
c) Salty and fresh

2. What shape is an arcuate delta?
a) Triangular
b) Square
c) Pointed

3. How do mangrove trees trap mud?
a) With their roots
b) With their leaves
c) With their seeds

4. How do mudskippers 'skip'?
a) With their fins
b) With skipping ropes
c) With their tails

Which fish is good at skipping?

Mudskippers (right) are finger-sized fish that live in mangrove swamps and mudflats all around the Indian and Pacific Oceans, from Africa to Polynesia. Whenever the tide goes out, they wriggle their tails and 'skip' across the mud or climb mangrove trees using their stumpy fins. When they are out of water, they breathe air that is trapped within their gill chambers. Some mudskippers claim territories, building low mud walls that keep their rivals out and stop seawater draining away at low tide.

27

Lakes

Lakes are water-filled hollows, varying in size, in the surface of the land. Most of these hollows were gouged out by huge glaciers and ice sheets, but some were formed by movements deep inside Earth's crust. Rivers sometimes become lakes when they come up against a barrier that acts like a dam.

Which lakes are formed by Earth's movements?

The world's deepest lakes were formed by movements and volcanic activity beneath Earth's crust, or skin, that caused the crust to crumple or crack. In places, deep cracking of the crust caused huge blocks of land to drop below the level of the surrounding land, creating steep-sided valleys called rift valleys. Over time, water filled up parts of the valleys, creating long, deep rift lakes (left).

Rift lake
Volcanic activity causes cracks in rock
Land slips down

What are the 'Great Lakes'?

The five large lakes (Superior, Michigan, Huron, Erie and Ontario) spanning the border of the USA and Canada are called the 'Great Lakes' (inset left). The water from Lake Erie plunges over the Niagara Falls before reaching Lake Ontario. Lake Superior is the second largest stretch of inland water in the world, after the Caspian Sea, and the largest and deepest of the Great Lakes. Its surface area, at more than 82,000 square kilometres, is almost double the size of Switzerland (inset left). Lake Superior is so large that the wind whips up its surface over great distances and forms huge waves, which produce sea-like conditions. Large ships (left) transport goods to and from the many ports on the Great Lakes.

CANADA
Lake Superior
Lake Huron
Lake Michigan
Lake Ontario
Lake Erie
USA
Switzerland

What are volcanic lakes?

Volcanic activity can form lakes in many ways. A lake may be formed when the solidified core, or 'plug', of an old volcano sinks downwards below the crater's rim, forming a hollow called a caldera. If the caldera fills with water it is called a crater lake. The largest caldera in the world is in Sumatra, Indonesia, and contains Lake Toba. Other lakes form when volcanic debris or lava dams a river and the water collects behind the dam to form a lake. Some volcanic lakes, such as Kawah Idjen (right) in Java, Indonesia, have a high measure of powerful acids in their water. Acidic gases bubble up through cracks in the lake-bed from the volcano below and dissolve in the water. Living things cannot survive in such highly acidic water, and people can be badly burned if they touch it.

Which lake is the deepest?

Lake Baikal (inset right), Siberia, plunges to 1,637 metres and is the world's deepest lake. In terms of surface area, it ranks sixth in the world. Lake Baikal contains around one fifth of all the unfrozen freshwater on Earth – 336 rivers and streams flow into it. During the Siberian winter, parts of the lake freeze and local people use the ice as a highway (right). Of the great variety of wildlife in the lake, three-quarters of the species are found nowhere else on Earth, including the Baikal seal – the world's only freshwater seal.

1,637 m

SIBERIA

Lake Baikal

MONGOLIA

Quick-fire Quiz

1. When was the last ice age?
a) 1 million years ago
b) 18,000 years ago
c) 5,000 years ago

2. How are the world's deepest lakes formed?
a) By glaciers
b) By Earth's movements
c) By beavers

3. How many rivers flow into Lake Baikal?
a) 400
b) 336
c) 556

4. How many Great Lakes are there?
a) 5
b) 9
c) 16

What are swamps and marshes?

A swamp is a cross between a lake and land. Its waters are usually very shallow and still, and yet lots of special kinds of trees and plants can be found growing in the water. The Everglades, in Florida, USA, is an enormous swamp, covering 10,600 square kilometres.

A marsh is drier than a swamp and water cannot always be seen, but the ground and the plants that grow in it are always soggy or heavily waterlogged. A marsh rarely has trees.

Swamp

Marsh

Which lakes are formed by the action of glaciers?

About 18,000 years ago, during the last ice age, ice sheets and glaciers covered much larger areas of land than they do now. As the ice moved over the land, it scoured great dips into the ground. When the climate warmed up and the ice melted, water filled these dips to form lakes such as the lochs of Scotland. High in the mountains, circular hollows called cirques (right), scraped out by the huge weight of ice at the head of glaciers, filled with water and became lakes. Other lakes formed when debris left behind by melting glaciers formed dams, which sometimes trapped water behind them.

Cirque

Head of glacier

Water Under the Ground

When rain falls some of it runs straight into rivers or lakes – but most of it soaks through the soil to rocks below. If the rock will not let the rain pass through (permeate), an underground river may form, flowing on top of the rock. Where the rain can flow through the rock, pockets of water called 'aquifers' develop. Over time, soft rocks, such as limestone, can be worn away by underground water and huge tunnels and caves may form.

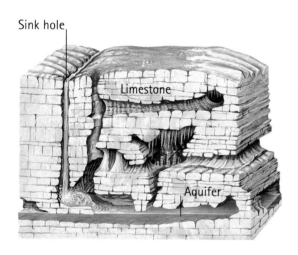

Sink hole

Limestone

Aquifer

What are stalactites and stalagmites?

As water drips from the roof of a limestone cave, it dissolves the minerals in the rocks. Some of the water in the drips evaporates, leaving the minerals behind. Over hundreds of years, these build up into icicle-shaped stalactites, which hang down from the cave roof (right). Stalagmites build up from water drips that splash onto the floor of the cave. Sometimes a stalactite and a stalagmite meet in the middle to form a pillar.

What is an aquifer?

An aquifer is a layer of rock or sediment through which water moves easily. Good aquifers include sandstone, chalk and limestone (above). These rocks are said to be 'porous' because there are tiny gaps, or pores, between the grains of rock through which water can flow. Some aquifers have been filling up for thousands of years and are like huge underground reservoirs. Wells are often drilled into these rocks and the water pumped out, although ancient aquifers can soon run dry.

What is an artesian well?

Sometimes an aquifer is sandwiched in a basin between two layers of 'impermeable' rock – rock that will not allow water to pass through. Because of the weight of the water pushing down from the sides of the basin, the base of the aquifer is under pressure. If a well is bored here, the water will gush out by itself. This is called an artesian well – the first well of this kind was dug by the Romans in Artesium, France.

Rain

Aquifer

Artesian well

Impermeable rock

Impermeable rock

How do caves and caverns form?

Cracks in limestone rock may be eaten away by rainwater to leave a deep, vertical shaft called a sink hole or a swallow hole. Water may flow down the sides of the hole to form spectacular underground waterfalls, often hundreds of metres deep. Underground water also dissolves limestone rock to form caves and caverns (left). Cave explorers enter these caves by climbing down large sink holes called potholes. The longest cave system in the world lies under the Mammoth Cave National Park in Kentucky, USA. It is over 530 kilometres long and has more than 60,000 sink holes.

What makes a geyser gush?

A geyser is a type of hot spring that regularly shoots out spectacular fountains of water and steam. Geysers occur in volcanic areas where hot rocks lie near to the surface. The rocks heat underground water to boiling point. As the water boils, its pressure rises, forcing the cooler water above it into a column up to 500 metres tall (right). Some geysers, such as Old Faithful in Yellowstone National Park, USA, reliably erupt every hour or so. Other geysers may have weeks or months between eruptions.

How does an oasis form?

An oasis is a moist, fertile area of a desert where an aquifer is close to the surface. The water often comes from rain that falls on mountains that are hundreds of kilometres away, before draining below the desert. A fault or crack above the aquifer (left) may allow this water to reach the surface naturally, or a well may sometimes be dug to deliberately create an oasis.

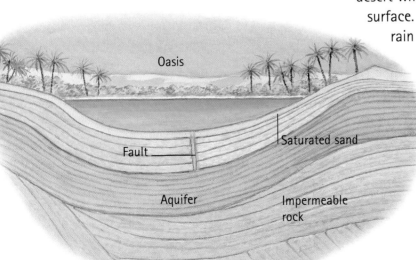

Oasis

Fault

Saturated sand

Aquifer

Impermeable rock

People, Oceans and Rivers

People have always had a close relationship with Earth's waters. Fish from the oceans have been a valuable food source for thousands of years and fresh river-water is vital for drinking, washing and irrigating our crops. People also use water for transport, trade, holidays and watersports. The awesome power of waves, tides and fast-flowing rivers has more recently been harnessed to give us electricity – while oil and minerals are mined from the sea-bed.

Are fish frozen at sea?

Huge factory fishing ships (above) stay at sea for months at a time and catch huge amounts of fish. In one day, they can catch more than 600 tonnes of fish, which have to be preserved until the ship gets back to port. First, the fish are gutted, cleaned and filleted. The guts are turned into fish-meal or fish-oil for fertilizers or animal feed – and stored in bags. The filleted fish are compressed into blocks of seafood paste and are rapidly frozen and packaged. They are then stored in a refrigerated hold. Nothing is wasted!

How do people use water for irrigation?

Since the time of the Ancient Egyptians, people have used various devices to lift river-water onto their fields to water their crops. In Egypt today, farmers still use the same simple but effective devices, such as the Archimedes screw and shadoof (left), that have been around for thousands of years. The Archimedes screw is like a corkscrew inside a tube. By turning the screw many times, a large amount of water can be lifted with little effort. In many countries low walls are built around fields to hold in the water, and sluicegates control the flow to the fields. Today, electric pumps are also used to transport water from rivers to the fields.

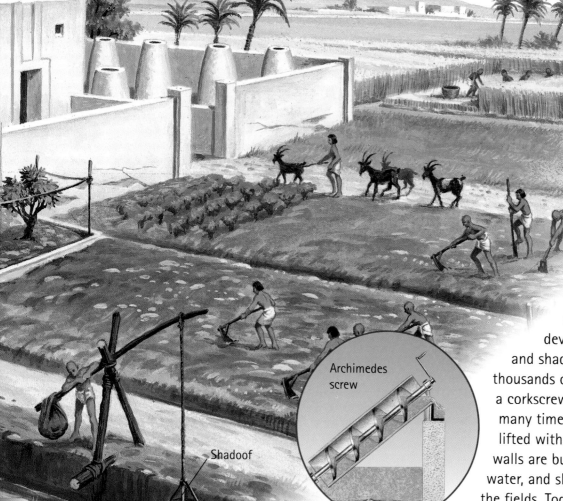

Archimedes screw

Shadoof

Where does oil come from?

Oil comes from the remains of tiny sea creatures that once thrived in Earth's ancient oceans. Over millions of years, heat and pressure have changed these remains into oil. Today, although the pattern of land and sea is very different, about two-fifths of our oil comes from under the sea. To bring it to the surface, huge drilling platforms or rigs (right) are towed out to the edge of the continental shelf where they drill wells 900 to 5,000 metres into the sea-bed.

Quick-fire Quiz

1. How deep are most offshore oil wells?
a) 900–5,000 m
b) 100–500 m
c) 5,000–20,000 m

2. What is power generated from water called?
a) Aquaelectricity
b) Hydroelectricity
c) Turbine power

3. How much fish can a factory ship catch each day?
a) 400 tonnes
b) 600 tonnes
c) 800 tonnes

4. Where does oil come from?
a) From deep-sea vents
b) From the remains of tiny sea creatures
c) From ancient fossilized trees

What pollutes the oceans?

Pollution has had a disastrous effect on many coastlines and land-locked seas. City sewage, chemical and industrial waste, and farmers' pesticides and fertilizers all find their way into Earth's seas and oceans. On the open ocean, tonnes of waste and rubbish is thoughtlessly thrown overboard from ships every day. But oil is one of the major pollutants of the oceans. It comes from ships illegally cleaning their oil tanks with seawater, and from tragic accidents such as when a tanker runs aground and spills its load (right). Another threat to the health of our oceans comes from the radioactive pollution of coastal nuclear power stations and sunken or damaged nuclear submarines.

Why do people dam rivers?

Dams are very strong, thick walls built across rivers to hold back the water (right). The water can then be released gradually to prevent flooding downstream. The water from the dam's reservoir can also be used to drive turbines and generate electricity. Such hydroelectric power stations do not pollute the environment and use a resource that will never run out. The only drawbacks are that a large area behind the dam must be flooded, and that changing the natural flow of water in a river can cause floods or droughts in other areas.

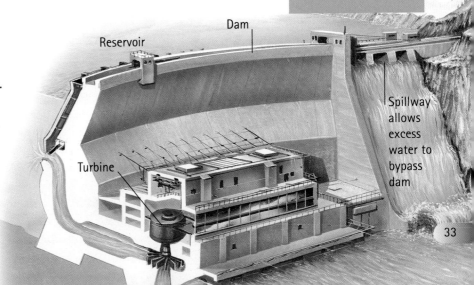

Reservoir

Dam

Turbine

Spillway allows excess water to bypass dam

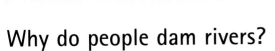

Watercraft

People have sailed the seas and oceans since the earliest times. Their first ships were wooden and powered by oars and sails. Much later, came metal ships with steam and diesel engines. Today there is an incredible variety of watercraft from jet-skis to enormous cargo ships. Some ships zoom across the ocean at high speed, while nuclear submarines lurk far below.

How does a submarine dive and surface?

A submarine dives underwater or rises to the surface by filling large tanks with water or air. If the tanks are filled with water, the submarine becomes heavier than the water around it, and sinks down. When it has reached the chosen depth, the valves that let water into the tanks are closed and the submarine stays at that depth. For the submarine to surface, air is pumped into the tanks – forcing the water out and making the submarine light enough to rise. Modern nuclear-powered submarines are totally self-contained, even recycling the air that the crew breathes. In this way, they can stay submerged for as long as their food supplies last.

A submarine floats when its tanks are full of air

To dive, the air is allowed to escape and water fills the tanks

To rise, air is pumped back into the tanks

What sorts of watercraft are used for water sports?

People take part in many water sports on rivers, lakes and the sea. Windsurfers zoom across the water on sailboards, while canoeists race their fibreglass canoes through the surf or down white-water rivers. For those in search of speed, streamlined powerboats can travel incredibly fast. Some racing boats even have aircraft engines and have set world records for speed. Jet-skis first went on sale in Japan in 1979, and the latest models (left) can zip along at speeds of up to 105 km/h.

What are container ships?

Container ships (below) carry all kinds of goods in large metal boxes called containers. Each container is a standard size – about 12 metres long and 2.5 metres wide, so they can be easily stacked onboard the ship. Each ship holds many thousands of containers, which can be loaded and unloaded from trains and lorries by cranes at the side of the dock. Three-quarters of the hull of a fully-loaded container ship is under the water, so it can only sail into deep-water harbours. The biggest container ships are so large that they need about eight kilometres in which to stop and a circle of over 1.6 kilometres to turn in.

What large wooden ships were driven by oars?

Among the most successful of the first ships built by early civilizations, were the galleys of the Phoenicians and Greeks and the longships of the Vikings (right). All these ships were low and narrow. Usually rigged with a single mast and a square sail, they were also equipped with rows of oars. This design made the ships particularly versatile, as they could sail across the sea to another country, be rowed up rivers and slip into shallow, sheltered harbours. When on raiding-trips, the Vikings would fix their painted shields to the side of the boat and use the oars for maximum speed. Viking cargo ships were similar to the longship in shape, but higher and wider. The largest of these could carry up to 38 tonnes of cargo.

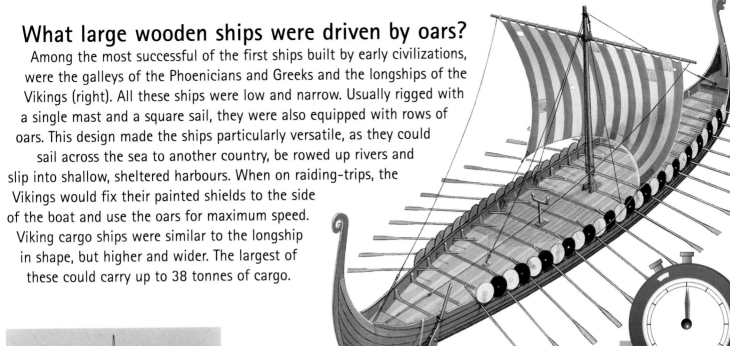

How does a hydrofoil work?

Hydrofoils (left) are ships that 'fly' through the water on underwater 'wings' called foils. The foils are attached to the ship by means of stilts. When the ship moves forward under power, the foils produce a lifting force – just as an aeroplane's wings do in the air. As the boat gathers speed, the hull is lifted clear of the water. Because the foils slice through the water with so little drag, hydrofoils can travel at speeds of up to 148 km/h.

Quick-fire Quiz

1. How much of a loaded container ship is under the water?
a) A half
b) A quarter
c) Three-quarters

2. What does a submarine need to do before it can surface?
a) Fill its tanks with water
b) Fill its tanks with air
c) Fire its torpedoes

3. Which kind of ship has wings?
a) A hydrofoil
b) A hovercraft
c) A catamaran

4. How large is a standard container?
a) 10 m x 5.5 m
b) 12 m x 6 m
c) 12 m x 2.5 m

Ocean Adventures

For tens of thousands of years, people have explored the oceans in search of new lands in which to settle and goods to trade. Today, ships cross the oceans at previously unimaginable speeds, while underwater craft explore the mysterious world below the waves. Yet, even with the help of submersibles, we still know less about the bottom of the ocean than we do about the surface of the Moon.

How deep can submersibles dive?

Submersibles are small underwater craft, built to withstand the crushing pressure deep beneath the ocean. One of the most successful is the American *Alvin* (right). It has made thousands of dives since it was built in 1964, carrying three people to depths of 4,500 metres. One of *Alvin's* most spectacular discoveries was that of deep-sea vents in the 1970s. But the *Alvin* is not the deepest-diving submersible. The US *Sea Cliff*, the Russian *Mir*, the French *Nautile* and the Japanese *Shinkai* can all dive to 6,000 metres, and so can explore everywhere except for the deepest of ocean trenches.

How long can scuba divers stay underwater?

Scuba stands for 'self-contained underwater breathing apparatus'. It was invented in 1943 by Frenchmen Jacques Cousteau and Emile Gagnan. Scuba divers carry tanks filled with air on their backs (below) and can dive for about an hour. Scuba divers can move freely because they carry their own air supply and do not have to wear cumbersome and heavy diving suits.

Jacques Cousteau

How did early people explore the oceans?

Although we have no information on the earliest sea-going vessels, we know that people crossed from South-east Asia to Australia and New Guinea at least 40,000 years ago. From about 1500 BC, Polynesian sailors settled on all the main islands in the middle of the Pacific Ocean within a triangle bounded by Hawaii, New Zealand and Easter Island. It is believed they used two canoes fixed together with a platform in the middle (left), to transport passengers, animals and plants across the ocean.

Which was the first ship to cross the Atlantic under steam power?

Although the first steamer to cross the Atlantic was the *Savannah* in 1819 – it sailed most of the way. Not until 1838 did a small, 700-tonne paddler, the *Sirius* (left), complete the whole journey under steam power. During the last part of the 19-day voyage, however, the *Sirius* ran out of coal and had to burn its cargo! Brunel's *Great Western* began its crossing four days after the *Sirius*, but arrived in New York just a few hours later, thanks to the efforts of the crew who kept the engines running at full speed night and day.

Who first sailed around the world alone?

The first person to sail around the world alone was Joshua Slocum. He set sail aboard his home-built craft, the *Spray*, in 1898 and completed the 73,600 kilometres in 1,158 days – stopping several times on the way. In 1969, Robin Knox-Johnson became the first person to sail around the world alone non-stop. He took 312 days and one hour to travel 48,197 kilometres in his yacht *Suhaili*.

How are satellites used to explore oceans today?

Nowadays, the oceans can be explored without travelling on or under the ocean. High above Earth, satellites in space are studying the oceans – constantly monitoring surface temperature, the speed and direction of currents, sea level, wave height, sea ice and even levels of plant life. This information helps scientists to understand more about how the oceans work and is useful to engineers seeking new offshore gas and oil reserves. Satellites also send signals to ships' computers (right), helping them to plot their positions accurately.

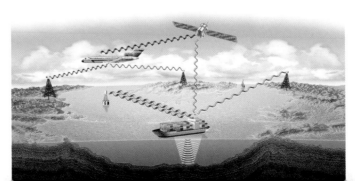

Ocean and River Facts

Oceans dominate the surface of Earth. The Pacific Ocean alone covers more area than all the continents put together. Key facts about some of the world's best-known rivers, lakes and oceans are recorded here.

Atlantic Ocean

- **Area:** 82,000,000 square kilometres. Earth's second largest ocean.
- **Average depth:** 3,330 metres.
- **Maximum depth:** 9,144 metres.
- **Volume:** 311,930,000 cubic kilometres.
- **Ocean currents:** Gulf Stream, Labrador Current, North Atlantic Current, Equatorial Current, Canaries Current and Brazil Current.
- **Special features:** Mid-Atlantic Ridge is the world's largest mountain range. Has the most shallow seas, such as the Gulf of Mexico, the Caribbean Sea and the Mediterranean Sea.

Pacific Ocean

- **Area:** 166,000,000 square kilometres. Earth's largest ocean.
- **Average depth:** 4,280 metres. Earth's deepest ocean.
- **Maximum depth:** 11,022 metres in the Challenger Deep of the Marianas Trench.
- **Volume:** 724,000,000 cubic kilometres.
- **Ocean currents:** North Equatorial Current, North Pacific Current, California Current, Kuroshio Current, Oyashio Current, Alaska Current, South Equatorial Current, West Wind Drift, Peru Current, East Australia Current and Equatorial Countercurrent.
- **Special features:** The so-called 'ring of fire' of volcanic activity around its edge. Mid-ocean ridges include the East Pacific Rise, Galapagos Rise and Chile Rise.

Antarctic Ocean

- **Area:** 35,000,000 square kilometres.
- **Average depth:** 4,000 metres.
- **Maximum depth:** 7,235 metres.
- **Volume:** 140,000,000 cubic kilometres.
- **Ocean currents:** Antarctic Circumpolar Current – transporting 130 million cubic metres of water per second, or ten times the flow of all the world's rivers put together.
- **Special features:** Sea ice. Four million square kilometres are permanently frozen and, in winter, a further 21,000,000 square kilometres freeze over.

Indian Ocean

- **Area:** 73,600,000 square kilometres. Earth's third largest ocean.
- **Average depth:** 3,890 metres.
- **Maximum depth:** 7,450 metres.
- **Volume:** 292,131,000 cubic kilometres.
- **Ocean currents:** South Equatorial Current, West Australia Current, Agulhas Current, North Equatorial Current and Equatorial Countercurrent.
- **Special features:** Y-shaped mid-ocean ridge. Climate dominated by monsoon winds. Many coral islands.

Arctic Ocean

- **Area:** 14,956,000 square kilometres. Earth's smallest ocean.
- **Average depth:** 990 metres. Earth's shallowest ocean.
- **Maximum depth:** 5,502 metres.
- **Volume:** 17,000,000 cubic kilometres.
- **Ocean currents:** Transarctic Current.
- **Special features:** Four minor basins and three ocean ridges. 10,000–50,000 icebergs drift south each year, taking with them two per cent of the ocean's water. In winter, sea ice – with an average thickness of 3–3.5 metres – covers 15 million square kilometres of the ocean.

River Nile
- **Length:** 6,695 kilometres. The longest river in the world.
- **Location:** White Nile flows through Uganda, Sudan and Egypt. Blue Nile flows through Ethiopia, Zaire, Kenya, Tanzania, Rwanda and Burundi.
- **Sources:** Lake Victoria (White Nile) and Lake Tana (Blue Nile).
- **Drainage basin:** 3,349,000 square kilometres.
- **Average discharge:** 3,000 cubic metres per second.
- **Special features:** Aswan Dam holds back one of the world's largest artificial lakes – Lake Nasser.

River Amazon
- **Length:** 6,440 kilometres. The second longest in the world.
- **Location:** Brazil.
- **Sources:** Many sources in the Andes mountains.
- **Drainage basin:** More than seven million square kilometres.
- **Average discharge:** 180,000 cubic metres per second. This flow reduces the saltiness of the Atlantic up to 160 kilometres offshore.
- **Special features:** At its mouth, the River Amazon is 240 kilometres wide.

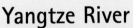

Yangtze River
- **Length:** 6,418 kilometres. The third longest river in the world.
- **Location:** China.
- **Source:** Mount Gelandandong, Tibet.
- **Drainage basin:** 1,959,000 square kilometres.
- **Average discharge:** 34,000 cubic metres per second.
- **Special features:** Large ships can reach 1,100 kilometres upriver. Passes through three gorges with walls as high as 1,000 metres.

Lake Victoria
- **Area:** 69,480 square kilometres. The second largest freshwater lake in the world.
- **Depth:** 82 metres.
- **Volume:** 2,760 cubic kilometres.
- **Coastline:** 3,220 kilometres.
- **Tributaries:** 22 rivers and streams.
- **Special features:** Has over 200 species of fish.

Lake Baikal
- **Area:** 31,500 square kilometres.
- **Depth:** 1,637 metres. The deepest lake in the world.
- **Volume:** 23,000 cubic kilometres.
- **Coastline:** 2,100 kilometres.
- **Tributaries:** 336 rivers and streams.
- **Special features:** At 25–50 million years old, it is believed to be the world's oldest lake. Contains 20 per cent of the world's freshwater. The sediment on the lake-bed is estimated to be more than seven kilometres deep. Provides a habitat for more than 1,200 animal species – three-quarters of which are found nowhere else, including the world's only freshwater seal.

Lake Superior
- **Area:** More than 82,100 square kilometres. The largest freshwater lake in the world.
- **Depth:** 147 metres.
- **Volume:** 12,100 cubic kilometres.
- **Coastline:** 4,385 kilometres.
- **Tributaries:** 20 rivers and streams including the Nipigon River and St Louis River.
- **Special features:** One of the five 'Great Lakes' of North America. Second only to Lake Baikal in volume – contains ten per cent of the world's freshwater.

Index

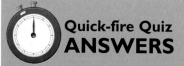

Quick-fire Quiz ANSWERS

Page 5 Water in our World
1. b   2. b   3. a   4. b

Page 7 World Oceans
1. b   2. a   3. b   4. b

Page 9 Seas of the World
1. c   2. c   3. c   4. a

Page 11 The Ocean Floor
1. a   2. a   3. b   4. b

Page 13 Islands and Reefs
1. c   2. b   3. b   4. c

Page 15 Ocean Currents
1. b   2. a   3. b   4. c

Page 17 Oceans and Climate
1. b   2. b   3. a   4. a

Page 19 Waves and Tides
1. a   2. a   3. a   4. c

Page 21 Coasts
1. c   2. a   3. b   4. c

Page 23 A River's Journey
1. b   2. c   3. c   4. c

Page 25 River Landscapes
1. b   2. a   3. c   4. c

Page 27 Where Rivers Meet ...
1. c   2. a   3. a   4. c

Page 29 Lakes
1. b   2. b   3. b   4. a

Page 31 Water Under the Ground
1. b   2. a   3. a   4. a

Page 33 People, Oceans and Rivers
1. a   2. b   3. b   4. b

Page 35 Watercraft
1. c   2. b   3. a   4. c

Page 37 Ocean Adventures
1. b   2. c   3. a   4. b